THE LADY IN THE BOTTLE

The Lady
In The Bottle

Rozanna Lilley

THE **BLACK SPRING**
PRESS GROUP

First published in 2023
by Eyewear Publishing Ltd.
an imprint of Black Spring Publishing Group
United Kingdom

Typeset with graphic design by Edwin Smet

ISBN 978-1-913606-69-5

*The editor has generally followed Australian spelling and punctuation
at the author's request.*

BLACKSPRINGPRESSGROUP.COM

For Neil, who gave me a DVD
set of the complete first season of I Dream of Jeannie
all those Christmases ago.

TRAILER

In the 1960s, I watched *I Dream of Jeannie* (1965-70)
on the black and white TV set in my family's lounge
room in Perth, Western Australia. I loved everything
about the show. Like other little girls around the
globe, I imagined living inside a sumptuous bottle,
reclining on velvet cushions. I thought about how
great it would be to marry an astronaut, to live in my
own home in Cocoa Beach, to be as glamorous as
Barbara Eden. Most of all, I longed for magic powers.
In my 50s, my husband gave me a DVD set of the
first series of this enduring fantasy sitcom. I began
watching the series over again as an adult woman.
This time around my reactions were different. I felt
disturbed by the outlandish Orientalism and outraged
by the predictable sexism of a story arc structured
around Jeannie's desperation to marry her Master.
Nevertheless, the show still held me in thrall. Perhaps
this is partly the simple pull of nostalgia. But maybe
it also has something to do with the inventiveness
of the plots and the many surprising, even uncanny,
moments. This series is intended as both fan poetry
and critique. Each poem corresponds to an episode
in the first series and takes its title, penned by Sidney
Sheldon, from that episode.

TABLE OF CONTENTS

THE LADY IN THE BOTTLE

I conjured him a falcon
windborne it hovered
circling my forsaken isle
talons curving a steely embrace

It wasn't enough

I offered a galley
its slender hull parting the ocean
steady oars sounding
our twinned heartbeat

But there's no pleasing a man
inflated by a red-hot NASA jumpsuit

A stowaway, I slipped on his business shirt
inhaling starched ambition until
bribed by a black pearl
I free-dived, deep harvesting
shards of stoppered silence

Later we laughed
levitating in the living-room   insouciantly horizontal
I saw the potted palm
                the Pierrot painting
                        the primitive bric-a-brac

It was always my hand scratching S-O-S

MY HERO?

The splashback's awash with groceries
freshly laminated love bursting
from brown paper bags
shortchanged by the solitary promise
of a space-age TV dinner

If he knew what it cost to return
that Baghdad sky indigo blazing
the market fresh-pressed
helter-skelter stalls
offering the known world

Finally transported home
to a two-bit studio lot
        a flimsy set-up

In Cocoa Beach I lap the chlorinated tides
the neighbours know we can't afford
my backstroke lazily grazing the charred moon

It's nearly dinnertime
he's waiting for Miss Galaxy to knock

The slave auction is over
and all my shekels are scattered
carelessly poolside

GUESS WHAT HAPPENED ON THE WAY TO THE MOON

We're all stowaways
on a DIY survival mission
walking Skull Flat in stockinged feet
winding up with saddle sores
winding down with a vodka martini
on the rocks

It's 110 in the shade
our walkie-talkies crackling
with mile after mile of
mirages swift buckling
          a blonde trickster in a nomad's tent
          a puma suspended mid-leap
the blink of a kohl-rimmed eye

Dr Bellows' stethoscope
hangs idly from forgiving pockets

The fiancée's portrait is
hidden in the teak bureau
her brunette beauty
encased in folds of
freshly laundered harem pants

I'd prefer the moon
to a weekend in Miami

Roger that

THE MARRIAGE CAPER

I offered
       to be a brunette
       serve figs at your nuptial bedside
       make myself small

Blinking, I became
       a Chinese houseboy
       tunic stiff with Fabulon

Intoxicated,
       he pulled my hair
       blood pooling at the dyed roots
(an awkward embrace)

She never
       anticipated thirst with iced water
       cubes slycracked with Kelvinator convenience
       or fixed a cheese sandwich from scratch
       the tethered goat bleating her milky refrain

If that bitch in blue chiffon ever returns
I'll flambé those frozen hors d'oeuvres

But sometimes I catch
a hint of her Chamade
lingering on the parquet stairs
the startling sheen of newly polished regret

G. I. JEANNIE

When I drove the jeep straight for the brickwall
I was thinking of the time He poured
the contents from the cutglass vase
             (rosepink petals scattered incautiously)
a vengeful waterfall cascading

Gasping, I remembered how I
phoned my Dad when I slammed into the
house   choosing the accelerator not the brake
Back then I still had faith in being rescued by a father
Figure that out

Later when Jack crashed his chariot
some sly Centurion swerved in a Pompeii bar to whisper
It *was your fault*
Parched, I sculled a shandy   choking
on civilian roadrage at a stranger's bridal shower

THE YACHT MURDER CASE

He might as well have pushed me overboard
doing time with a champagne cocktail
the fizz of infidelity fixing a Coppertone smile
Miss Ferguson's manicured fingers
deftly loosening a lazy jib

For this, he hoovered me up
trapped in an upright vacuum
       (beater-bar bruising svelte thighs)
listening to the persistent tock
       of the sunburst clock
chafing on canned laughter
       from the Silvertone Suburbanite
dustbag filtering calloused thoughts

It's sleeker to be a model
without attachments
to dim fluorescent yearning
but when the switch is finally flicked
the chord retracts
leaving a Teflon tryst
to smooth our chequered passage

Love sucks

STARBRIGHT

Everything is different in space
instead of a heartbeat, a roaring wind
our silvered suits shining with
wish-I-may and wish-I-mights
the hatch opened

If we ever get back to Cocoa Beach
I'll windex the coral lipstick
barnacled to his winged helmet
and fix a breakfast
of plover eggs and percolated coffee
            just the way he likes it

My typewriter carriage swings
back and forth tethering
            the swift flight of dragonflies
            the soft plash of falling nectar
            the steady hum of webspinners
            adrift in silken chambers

We no longer need a capsule
our umbilical line traces the wide horizon
tunnelling home

PRACTICE MAKES PERFECT

He said I resembled a fugitive from a costume party
It didn't sound like a compliment
Reflecting I sought refuge between the covers
of *Elite* magazine, learning about losers and how
to be modern   (slipperfetching is seriously passé)

Uncorked, I emerged in a midnight-blue beaded gown
tastefully accessorised   *You are beautiful*
Some days winning the battle is as easy as folding away
your harem pants and sipping Napoleon brandy

But all through that meal I could only think about
the time I hunted wild boar with Marco Polo
the shaft driven recklessly deep
his glossy tusks bathed in resplendent moonlight

THE MOVING FINGER

The anatomical chart fluttered
in the vacant hush
a desert wind gusting the soundstage
an inky arrow pointing
to the hollow space that holds the heart
arteries scarlet with insistent life

I saw him lost in the cover of *Movie Fame*
a bouffant brunette sultry with cultured pearls
I knew I could step inside her spotlight

Recited Omar Khayyám to a starstruck crew
(quiet-on-set)
recalled our last *tête-à-tête* in Nishapur
the quatrains falling lucid from those cursive lips
as Halley's comet streaked the velvet-crushed sky

But the screentest showed only empty space –
my vampiric invisibility forever caught
in celluloid arrhythmia

DJINN AND WATER

Great grandfather's land is rank with life:
four ruby-stained rivers running to the foaming sea
freshly fallen pomegranates weave the surface
as rose-ringed parakeets dip driving currents

In his test tube bower
my Master strives to conquer physics
to make saltwater fresh
he labours at his desk –
a billowing mushroom cloud
framed for inspiration
hangs its ektachrome promise
on the freshly plastered wall

Taking the wheel of his Pontiac convertible
my finger flips the Rand McNally index
until, arriving at my *locus amoenus*,
I carve donuts in the dreary street
skidmarks graphing the matted astroturf
each evergreen blade bent with unrequited longing

WHATEVER BECAME OF BABY CUSTER?

On our private patio, we levitate
sweating in this season's swimsuits –
a pellmell scattering of travertine pavers
safeguarding against the fall

The bugle sounds *Revelry*
It's Custer's last call!
Do you think I'm some sort of schizophrenic?
he shouts,
a one-child orbit spinning in a
padded ezy chair

His mother feared he was lost in space
but fastforward and you'll find
he was only hanging   heartbroken
at the edge-of-town
mesmerised by the centrifugal force
of a fat lady
forgetting to ever phone home

At plot's end we're all novices
at celestial navigation
jiving with Galileo   blindsided
by carnival's ribald dark

WHERE'D YOU GO GO?

He was captured by a puff piece
in the *Cocoa Beach Herald*
about the barefoot waterskiing of some
speed junkie beauty queen

Retaliating with a mink stole and a bouffant updo,
I knelt to tie the shoelaces of his best friend
never guessing that together
they'd hatched a date rape battle plan

When my Master kissed my champagne parched mouth,
he mistook bare-teeth for simian smile
moaning *I'm only human*
as his sliderule calculated the angle of orbital re-entry

Afterwards I dreamed
of aerospace workers salvaging derelict prototypes,
gently polishing each tarnished find
their splayed toes pirouetting on burning sand

RUSSIAN ROULETTE

When the kitchen wallpaper peeled back –
burnt orange geraniums blooming on brown plaid –
their scrawled numbers reappeared
Abigail to Zelda
papermate memorials of Smirnoff-fuelled calls
each clammering for attention

That's how we used to live
a mistress was no better than a master
they all start with a chauffeured Rolls Royce
and end up begging for love

Sometimes along the way
there's a slap in an elevator
            waiting for room-service
a bellhop with a grainy thoughtograph
pacing the receding hallways
of the Miami International Hotel

Once you've walked in space
your footwork obediently traces
the steps of a toxic waltz

WHAT HOUSE ACROSS THE STREET?

My TV mother is echolalic
each recycled phrase a jingled testament
Darling, blondes do have more fun

Dad is a lifesize standup
custom finished with flame retardant
You know you're soaking in it

He momentarily takes the lead
as the tin-foil phonograph plays
Waltz in Swing Time

No Fred and Ginger,
their halting box-step traces
a ragged faux romance

The cardboard cutout mansion is torn
straight from the pages of *American Home*
every dormer window and manicured hedge
sculpting perennial solidity

But when I blinked, there was only a vacant lot
dense with Arrowleaf
and the ballooning cupidity of Love-in-a-Puff

TOO MANY TONYS

My silver eye needle plucks
an invisible seam
corselet skeleton scaffolding
a reckless foam of hand-stitched lace

When that wedding march plays
I'll be ready

Meanwhile the timer is ticking
as the Betty Crocker angel cake
triumphantly rises
through a Visi-Bake door
leading to friend-zone purgatory

Your doppelgänger   the impatient bridegroom
moans suggestively
announces a year-long honeymoon
ardently kisses my arched swan neck

When I blink, he's reluctant to leave
He sees
          the stirred martini
          the ironed newspaper
          the way I fetch and carry

He may not be real
but he hovers in that half-world
a packet-mix promise refusing erasure

GET ME TO MECCA ON TIME

Has it really been 2000 years
since Jupiter and Mercury aligned?

A hand's splatter silhouetted
on butchers paper
and two pairs of ragged baby shoes
   scant remains

In this thieves' market
the bucket plunders a well so deep
that all I can see are stars

Bottle to Genie
Genie to Master
Master to Mecca
   we plead to try again

Rewind
a seaglass bottle on a beach
glints with clouded promise

Today's horoscope advises
bluntness could provoke blowback

I'm hitching a ride
on a one-hump camel
its rhythmic pitch and yaw
marking my solo pilgrimage
   a planetary precession guiding the way

THE RICHEST ASTRONAUT IN THE WHOLE WIDE WORLD

Browsing *A Beginner's Guide to Crewel Embroidery*
I overheard his lovelorn declaration
my cross-stitch interior turned topsy-turvy

Finders keepers he proclaimed
and that was that – kidnapped!

I pictured the layby tulle gown
my mothballed devotion

But it turned out he only wants
an Italian silk suit
some scantily clad servants
a seat on the stock exchange

We eat roast pheasant at every meal

When I turn back time
(the safe finally cracked)
I'll go back to Cocoa Beach
and pick up where I left off
a double strand of rayon floss conjuring
a leaping gazelle
       gobsmacked
             in mid-flight

IS THERE AN EXTRA JEANNIE IN THE HOUSE?

In Andromeda Inlet I've heard
wild roses riot
running through chattering forests
to milkwhite sands
their yellow petals scattered
in the wake
of manta rays and flying fish
drifting warm currents

My exile is
a living room
a handblown vase
a clutch of cheery blossoms
a sentinel of jet-black thorns

What kind of patriot says *no* to an astronaut?
When a fella walks all those miles out in space
megalomania's a given
If he needs to be called Master
recognise the understatement
He looped the moon and witnessed Earthrise

My only accomplishment –
an artfully arranged bouquet
skin scratched deep vermillion

NEVER TRY TO OUTSMART A GENIE

I'll be your Joan of Arc
trade my collar dress for coarse cloth
stoke rough-hewn remembrance
rerelease the final cut

When you try to shy away
I'll force your hands apart
and, sidewalk kneeling,
make you see my face

It's one daddy of a party
the dance band playing
Puppet on a String

But the guests have all gone home
before the final bang
on the big bass drum

Stateless, I'm confined to quarters

The Miami passport office
refused to recognise
a remixed Babylon born arsonist
gutter drunk crooning
> *I wonder if one day that*
> *you'll say that you care*

MY MASTER, THE DOCTOR

Be careful what you wish for
In Fantasyland
dreams do come true

I can make a silk purse
from a sow's ear   or
a virtuoso violinist
from an antiquated astronaut

The Queen of Hearts
does not bake tarts
She spreads your ribcage
suspending time

My advice is
check whose hand is
wielding the scalpel

Don't succumb to
a tumescent urge
to grope a woman in a
nurse's uniform

She's actually your surgeon

A gridiron incision only
momentarily stems
the incessant flow of years

Beneath the drawbridge
giant perch break
the saltwater surface
gasping for endling's breath

there is no bypass

JEANNIE AND THE KIDNAP CAPER

She sashays across the warehouse floor
barely able to breathe
in a cheongsam bursting
with scarlet peonies
teetering amongst makeshift towers

it's a set-up

Captain Nelson is hog-tied
waterboarding cues canned laughter
   can't you take an Oriental joke?

Hoh Lin Dai cuts his cruel bonds
serves drugged tea
makes awkward syntax promises
to spend long hours together

I've had enough
he's my Master, not her slave

I'm unversed in dialectics but note
that the sitcom audience nearly died
laughing
when the Cantonese princess-spy became
a shrieking sulphur-crested cockatoo

Maybe my jealousy was misplaced
she probably preferred
pashing Vincent Price *moumantai*

HOW LUCKY CAN YOU GET?

Venus reclines in her alcove
dreaming
beneath a three-arm chandelier
     she's plastered again

At the Buffalo Bar
an oversized olive swings
like a pendulum
pulsing the dripdry night

Here's another eager roller –
the slot machine
(on automatic payout) spills
a sea of dimes

The pit boss prowls
the broadloom floor
searching for spookers
     in this windowless country
     we make our own luck

I'm tired of orchestrating
other people's winning streaks
Liberty Bells tolling on repeat

Now that you're a Major
will I always be a minor?

Uncorked in a Reno flophouse
staring at bullhorns
as I shuffle a stacked deck

WATCH THE BIRDIE

We all know the traffic was
bumper-to-bumper
no one needs a hole-by-hole account

My advice is bend over
                          and
keep your knees together

Well, *hello* Major!

If you find yourself
stripped bare on the lawn
              ball still on the tee
gentlemen will excuse you

While Admiral Tugwell
fretfully cocks his wrists
(anchors aweigh)
little Jerry Barber relives
his par-saving putt at 17

When I compared
the Country Club to
the Hanging Gardens,
it was hyperbole

Like Queen Amytis
I'm fond of a
mountainous situation

But listen to an old pro
        when the grip whips
        from your hands
        the noose tightens

PERMANENT HOUSE GUEST

When my Master announced
that Dr Bellows had come
to stay I smashed
each dinnerplate
strewing shards of radioactive glaze

It's unsettling to host
a sofa surfing shrink
hunting an African elephant
tamed by Hollywood's jungle
in a bachelor's bedroom

Bellows licked his diagnostic
lips at pheasant-under-glass
but found the Californian
artichokes were poached
with moonshot nightmares

He said his mother
loved his younger brother
more and dreamed
of ways to stalk him
through the burgeoning bluegrass

A Cinesound cavalcade
of beating tom-toms and whistling bombs
finally forcing him out the door
my impatient ventriloquy
a slavegirl's victorious battle call

BETTER THAN A GENIE

She took his hand
tracing the oblique scar
that ran, like freedom,
over the neighbour's barbed-wire fence
towards the Everglades
          a slice of coiled remembrance

He glanced at the crystal ball
a reluctant scryer
the past returning
with a whoop-and-a-holler
that winded

When he found his breath
Chuck Yeager gazed back
cutting the tendon that
tethered him
to earth's unruly atmosphere

If she hadn't been a fraud
he might have seen
the Beechcraft flaming
on an Islamabad airfield
while Indira Gandhi gave Uncle Sam
the remaining finger

The glass abrasively etched
by the recursive promise
of a boy's own adventure

MY MASTER, THE GREAT REMBRANDT

The paint-by-numbers kit proclaims
Every man's a Rembrandt

While Ethel Merman tried her hand at 'Old Mill'
(the water wheel still turning)
J. Edgar Hoover donned
the laddered charm of 'Swiss Village'

My Master, unable to resist
the hodgepodge narcissism of
a plumed beret *and* a half-shaved poodle,
immodestly chooses 'Self Portrait in Oriental Attire'

Eager for a change of mood
I opt for 'Sunflowers'
that promiscuous promise of chrome yellow
is so *completely Vincent*

By the time the brushwork dries
the window frames a gibbous moon
hope hovering in the starry night
        a formulaic nocturne of picture perfect love

MY MASTER, THE THIEF

The silhouette suitcase stands by the door
holding only a pair of slippers
their tassels frayed by the passing whirl
of a caliph's court, my belly aching

I will not stay in a den of thieves

If I make it to Grand Rapids
unhooked
I'll post a vivid-filter photo
of the falls on Insta
and send a single sequin C-O-D

Then I'll book a table for one
twisting barefoot at Maxims
phone on silent

After you fix your coffee
(adding a sachet of Splenda)
try calling Alice –
you never can tell
she might still pick up for
technicolour romance

THIS IS MURDER

I stand in the centre of a great depression
a horned lark's solitary song tumbling
the dry gullies of the Gobi Desert
conjuring clouds pregnant with rain
to flood the vastness
a yacht's sail billowing surrender

I did it for you

In Bermuda I battled the Gulf Stream
piling snow in drifts so deep
petrels retreated *en masse*
to their earthy burrows
a popup ski lodge tricked out with antler
chandeliers filling the swirling sky

I did it for you

Hummingbirds feast on Alaskan pineapples
spiralled with permafrost

I did it for you

My only reward – your Sisyphean infidelity

MY MASTER, THE MAGICIAN

Abracadabra!
it's almost midnight
I listen for his footfall
the house chafing
in a haze of Saharan dust

Kalamazoo!
a monkey in a cardboard fez
pushes an empty pram
whiteface astronauts applauding
her grim pantomime

Presto!
the vanishing cane reveals
a posy of paper flowers
each crinkled
with garish sincerity

Some days I'm in the mood
to disappear
it's just a question
of who cracks first
I know he only wants
his eggs soft scrambled
his clownshoes polished
bright with amateur promise

But when you can
move vast mountains
and make the earth shake
Cocoa Beach is
a preposterous estate

I'LL NEVER FORGET WHAT'S HER NAME

Is this a waking dream?
I love you, Jeannie
I want to marry you
the final triumph
             in black & white

My slapstick victory –
a matching skirtsuit
a missing ring
a celebrant waiting
in the Sunset Studio wings

Ever since he uncorked my bottle
I've had the bends   locked
in a laugh-a-minute quartet
with a hapless headshrink &
a lecherous best friend

But a genie can never be
an astronaut's wife
I conjured a man-on-the-moon
his shining suit mirroring
my mortal ambitions

One blink and he is
(almost) forgotten
a vaudevillian chapter
of episodic need
in a story that never ends

CREDITS

My thanks to the literary journals in which 3 of the poems published here previously appeared: 'The lady in the bottle' (Tincture), 'Where'd you go go?' (Australian Poetry), 'What house across the street?' (Rabbit Poetry).